Sheikh Hasina

The Essence of Her World

An insight into a
Literary Politician

by Ashequn Nabi Chowdhury

Published by
Filament Publishing Ltd
16, Croydon Road, Beddington,
Croydon, Surrey CR0 4PA UK
+(0)20 8688 2598
www.filamentpublishing.com

@ 2021 Ashequn Nabi Chowdhury

ISBN 978-1-923623-77-7

The right of Ashequn Nabi Chowdhury
to be identified as the author of this work has been
asserted by him in accordance with the Designs
and Copyrghts Act 1988 Section 77.

All rights reserved
No portion of this work may be copies without the
prior written permission of the publishers.

Printed in the UK
Available worldwide
Photos: Courtesy to Saiful Islam Kallol
Covers of Sheikh Hasina's books
are courtesy of the publishers concerned

> "My thoughts, my writings are for the deprived masses, in the hope that they will inspire them into shaping new hope for themselves."

People and Democracy, Sheikh Hasina, Preface

THE AUTHOR

A post-graduate in Bengali language and literature, Ashequn Nabi Chowdhury, has been a journalist for over three decades, working at prominent news organisations including Bangladesh's premier English daily The Bangladesh Observer, The Financial Express, The New Age and the country's national news agency, Bangladesh Sangbad Sangstha (BSS).

Chowdhury has developed critical observation and writing skills through professional training courses and workshops in Bangladesh, Canada, China, Germany, India, New Zealand, and the United States. He extensively travelled to Asia, Australasia, Europe, and North America for writing stories.

Throughout his career, he has written for news media, international journals, and multinational organisations covering a range of topics. He has also written many literary pieces with the passion he developed while studying literature and continues to enjoy today.

Chowdhury has analysed the political philosophy, development strategies, and life perception of Sheikh Hasina, which she has expressed powerfully through her writings. 'The Essence of Her World' is the culmination of his research.

TABLE OF CONTENTS

Preface

Chapter One 1

Her empathy for others and attention to real-world situations with cautious, but caring eyes make her writings stand out.

Chapter Two 5

Between her return to Bangladesh and becoming prime minister, Sheikh Hasina established herself as an accomplished writer.

Chapter Three 19

In her writings she conveys a philosophy on how to guarantee development, democracy, secular values and peace.

Chapter Four 37

It is also a hallmark of her writings to reflect a deeper and more meaningful perspective on life.

Chapter Five 55

The Major Works of Sheikh Hasina

References 73

PREFACE

NOBODY understands Bangladesh more deeply than its long-serving prime minister, Sheikh Hasina. It is fortunate that she is an accomplished writer. Aside from politics, one of her strong suits is writing.

She has written many books on various subjects, such as politics, development, human rights, and the issues she considers to be most important in life.

Having read and analysed her wide-ranging and masterfully written books, one can certainly gain great insight into her life journey and the experiences of her country. She is unique among contemporary politicians for the way she connects ideas, writes with analytical vigour, and sheds light on life based on her own experiences.

This book— "The Essence of Her World"— celebrates Sheikh Hasina's writings, draws attention to the key themes of her works and offers a detailed account of her literary life.

Sheikh Hasina has presented an inspiring vision of Bangladesh and its role in the world. By exploring her written words, both as a person who has experienced a terrible tragedy and also as a prime minister who has served four terms, we discover the true spirit of Bangladesh.

CHAPTER ONE

Her empathy for others and attention to real-world situations with cautious, but caring eyes make her writings stand out.

IT IS NOT surprising that Sheikh Hasina's life is full of striking aspects. One of her many accomplishments is that she is a literary politician. Despite her hectic public life as the Bangladesh's only four-term Prime Minister and as the leader of the country's largest political party since returning from exile in the early 1980s, she has written several books to establish herself as a literary politician. Her creativity allows her to express ideas clearly and interpret incidents with great eloquence. Like any great author, her writings profoundly engage readers with the subjects she covers, the manner in which she uses them, and her positive outlook on life. For her, life is not about what she desires, but about what she has experienced.

In her works, she embodies the exceptional experiences with the essence of literature, as well as a genuine insight into the element of reality.

A strong literary streak runs in parallel to Sheikh Hasina's political career. There is also a clear connection between her conviction as a politician and as a writer. As a politician, she reaches out to people and gives them words of hope. Her writings reflect the same approach shining with warmth and compassion. Her empathy for others and attention to real-world situations with cautious, but caring eyes make her writings stand out. She does not belittle anyone's feelings, opinions, or beliefs.

She studied literature and enjoyed reading books, especially creative writings. She grew up in a book-loving environment thanks to her parents, who were avid readers. In her teens, Sheikh Hasina became acquainted with literary works in Bengali and throughout her studies at the University of Dhaka, she became more enamoured with the treasure of Bengali and world literatures. During those years, she read many novels, stories, and poems, particularly those about rural life. Bibhutibhushan Bandopadhyay's 'Pather Panchali' amazed her the first time she read it. Among her favourites were short stories of Rabindranath Tagore and the paintings of Zainul Abedin, especially those set in the rural context: "Bibhutibhushan's 'Pather Panchali' astonished me the first time I read it. …

Tagore's short stories, specially those set in the rural context, and the paintings of Zainul Abedin depicting rural Bengal are my favourites." [1]

In many of her writings, she describes how much she loves reading and to what extent books were part of her parents' lives: "Since 1949, my father has always kept a few selected books with him when he was in prison. After each jail term, he would donate most of the books to the prison library, except for some special collections. At the request of my mother, he took back the books, including works by Rabindranath, Sharatchandra, Nazrul and Bernard Shaw, all marked with the censor stamp by the jail authorities….. My mother would keep these books with great care... I was heartbroken as all those historic books were looted (by the Pakistani occupation force and their cohorts during 1971 War of Independence)." [2]

A central influence on Sheikh Hasina's literary and political career is her emotional and philosophical bond with her father Bangabandhu Sheikh Mujibur Rahman. As the eldest of five children, she used to spend more time with her father than her siblings. During their conversations, they would discuss politics, society, and plans for the country: "I used to spend more time with my father when I had the opportunity of having discussions on his plans for the country". [3]

As she grew up, Bangabandhu's Bengali nationalist ideals profoundly shaped her outlook on life and enabled her to embark on her journey. She draws inspiration from her father's speeches when she speaks. She also has literary aspirations influenced by Bangabandhu, who has been called the 'Poet of Politics'. Her unique leadership style stems from her strong bond with her father. Likewise, her literary achievements show the path she has followed, including the struggles she endured and the way she won the hearts and minds of people. A powerful intellect and ingenuity, as well as clarity and political perspectives, distinguish her literary style. She is a passionate writer who seeks to put into words her experiences as a woman growing up with her family, spending time with her father, and observing the world around her. With honesty and sincerity, she writes from the heart and weaves her observations and thoughts into words both as to how she believes they should be and as to how she wants them to be: "Writings that I do come from my heart.... I try to weave my observations and thoughts about a situation and an incident into words, both the way I think they should be and the way I want them to be."[4]

Her works demonstrate how she has overcome many internal and external challenges and how her individual persuasiveness, intelligence, and compassion began to emerge since she returned from exile.

CHAPTER TWO

Between her return to Bangladesh and becoming prime minister, Sheikh Hasina established herself as an accomplished writer.

SHEIKH HASINA'S return to Bangladesh after nearly six years in exile was a return to both her political life that started in her intermediate college days, and to her literary career, which began at Dhaka University. Besides, Bangladesh witnessed the beginning of a new chapter in its political history when she returned, and her speech on that historic day demonstrated both her political ideology and literary spirit.

The day was Sunday 17th May, 1981 -the most exciting day in Dhaka for years. Throughout the country people were tense in

anticipation of impending events.

The broad thoroughfare leading from Kurmitola Airport (now Hazrat Shahjalal International Airport) to Farmgate was full of people; jubilant yet cautious. Armed security personnel were on alert, with plainclothes agents of the intelligence services mingling with the crowd. They were constantly updating the higher authorities about the situation. Inside a highly secure cantonment house and surrounded by high-ranking officials in uniform, the top brass was stressed and anxious about what was happening outside and when it would end.

There was a quick sighting of a plane in the sky, and the crowds and security personnel watched it descend. The aircraft hovered for a short time before touching down at the airport. Higher authorities were immediately informed about the arrival of Air India's special flight from New Delhi via Kolkata with a very special passenger on board. She was none other than Sheikh Hasina, the eldest daughter of the Founding Father of Bangladesh, Bangabandhu Sheikh Mujibur Rahman. In the last half hour before landing, she glanced out the window to see the landscape of the country her father led to freedom.

When she caught a glimpse of the landscape perhaps at Tungipara, the place of her birth where her father lies in eternal rest, her eyes filled with tears and her heart burst with pain. Yet she fought back the pain and rekindled her determination to seek justice for her father, mother, brothers and other family members who were assassinated in the most brutal incident in Bangladesh's history.

As she left the aircraft, leaders of her political party, many of whom were close associates of her father, greeted her with high emotion and escorted her to a large reception arranged at Manik Mia Avenue, next to Jatiya Sangsad – the national parliament. People lined the road from Kurmitola to Manik Mia Avenue chanting "Joy Bangla" slogan openly for the first time after the gruesome assassination of her father along with most of her family in the early hours of 15 August 1975 by a handful of army renegades who invaded his residence as part of a strategically plotted coup. That event has scarred Bangladesh's history and led to a long period of political suffering.

The day Sheikh Hasina returns to Bangladesh resembles her father's homecoming, although they occurred over a decade apart. On the day of Bangabandhu's homecoming after spending solitary imprisonment in a Pakistan jail, tens of thousands of jubilant and excited people of all ages and communities gathered at the Tejgaon Old Airport and its surrounding areas, braving chilly weather and chanting "Joy Bangla". The day was later recalled by Sheikh Hasina in one of her writings as 'another historic day' for the people of Bangladesh. She reflects on how her father went straight to Suhrawardi Udyan upon returning to his beloved motherland from the death cell in Pakistan, and how emotional and glorious the re-union was: "The 10th of January 1972 is another historic day for the people of Bangladesh. The Father of the Nation returned to his motherland on this day and headed straight to Suhrawardi Udyan, where thousands of people from across the country had been jubilant since morning. He returned victorious to the same place from where he made his historic 7 March speech announcing Bangladesh's independence and Pakistani invading forces surrendered on 16 December 1971. When he reached his loved ones, it was an emotional reunion. A sense of triumph and pain flooded his heart as he stood in front of them." [5]

There was a similar frenzy of joy and excitement on Sheikh Hasina's homecoming day. She made an emotional yet powerful opening statement at the reception, setting the tone for the rest of her speech as well as her future plans: "I have come to stay among the people of Bangladesh," she pledged. Then she looked at the sea of people that surrounded her and continued: "I'm not a leader and I'm not here to be a leader of the Awami League."

As she spoke, you could have heard a pin drop. Those listening to the speech realised it went deeper than politics. Sheikh Hasina explained her intentions in a few words: "I wish to remain your sister, your daughter and an Awami League worker who adheres to Bangabandhu's ideals. I want to see justice. Those who killed my father, mother, brothers and their wives, as well as many others, should be brought to justice. As well, I hope to hold accountable those who caused the unbearable situation here in this country since 1975. Regardless of all differences, let's be united again. Victory is certain for us."

Sheikh Hasina concisely explained what she hoped to accomplish. She summoned the spirit of her father, who was a source of inspiration as she looked out over the thousands of people around her. On that day, the authorities intentionally turned off the street lights on Manik Mia Avenue, blanketing the entire area with darkness. Ignoring the darkness and inclement weather condition, thousands of people roared in response to her inspiring and appealing speech, chanting slogans like "Joy Bangla" and "Sheikh Hasina Zindabad." (Long Live Sheikh Hasina).

Following the reception, she along with a large crowd marched towards Dhanmondi 32, the historic house where her father, mother, brothers and their wives were murdered by the enemies of an independent Bangladesh. Sheikh Hasina intended to offer prayers inside the house for all the martyrs of 15 August 1975, but security denied her entry. In such a situation, she offered prayers on the road, joined by her supporters and party leaders. It was a crucial event in establishing herself as the heir to her father's legacy and the leader of the country's largest party. [6]

People soon came to regard her as a courageous and uncompromising leader, capable of freeing the country from the grip of Bangabandhu's killers. Her journey has been completely different since then - one involving millions of people while another involves exploring the world independently. However, it took Sheikh Hasina 15 years to bring her party back to power and become the country's prime minister. This was largely due to the military and quasi-military rule after 1975 that undermined democracy.

Between her return to Bangladesh and becoming prime minister, Sheikh Hasina established herself as an accomplished writer. Her writing continued even when she was confronted with much important work for the state or her party. This was true both when she was the head of the government and an opposition leader. Her most difficult years were between 1975 and 1996 when both politics and free-thinking were hard tasks. Yet she continued to write as well as to pursue the political struggle because of her love for the country and its people. From her writings of this period, we can see how she spearheaded the end of martial law in Bangladesh and freed the nation from the grip of autocracy.

It was during this period that she faced many challenges, including being arrested frequently for leading pro-democracy movements. There was even difficulty holding street rallies at that time due to the army-backed Ershad government's desperate efforts to suppress oppositions. The violent attack of musclemen supported by the state security forces on opposition political parties was a common scene in Dhaka and other cities. Sheikh Hasina addressed a rally in Dhaka during this difficult time where many party activists, supporters, and bystanders were severely injured by police. Among them was a street boy named Mannan. Sheikh Hasina saw him as she came down from the podium after her speech. Even though she had met street children before, this time Mannan was injured and in need of immediate medical attention, so she took the helpless street child to a clinic, arranged for his treatment, and brought him home.

Mannan was not the only one, many others like him were sheltered in her family homes in Dhaka and Tungipara. We find in her writings a touching story of Zulekha that portrays the eras of abuse against women characterised by child marriages, polygamy, misinterpretations of religious beliefs, and most significantly, lack of education and awareness about women's rights. Zulekha, however, was lucky enough to get shelter at Bangabandhu's village home. Otherwise, she and her children would have ended up on the city streets like many other women who were overabundant by their husbands or widowed early.

As her writings demonstrate, she has in many ways inspired oppressed people, such as street boy Noor Hossain who spoke out against systematic tyranny by Ershad's military government and was killed on 10 November in 1987. By describing Noor Hossain's story, Sheikh Hasina also illustrates her careful attention to the things and events around her:

"Up ahead was a young man, full-bodied, with a full crop of hair and possessed of a complexion that defined the Bengali physique. On his chest was written, in white, a slogan, 'Down with Autocracy'. And on his back, again in white, was the spirited message- 'Let Democracy Be Free'.... The image captured my attention very powerfully. At one point, he turned to me as if to show me what he was trying to convey. Then I asked my party workers to bring him to me. But he was fast losing himself into the crowd. Soon he was before me again. I remember asking him to put his shirt on so that he wouldn't put himself in danger and even be killed by police. Lowering his head toward me, he said: 'Apa, bless me, I'll sacrifice my life.'

Strongly opposing, I told him this wasn't what I needed. I no longer needed martyrs, instead I wanted to see the victorious warriors. [7]

The street children left her with such a lasting impression that she wrote a thought-provoking piece about them, asking why are they street children, and it became the title of the first book she wrote "Ora Tokai Keno"- Why are they Street

Children? The word 'Tokai' of the title article of this book is a reference to Bangladesh's most famous cartoon character created by eminent artist Rafiqun Nabi, best known as 'Ranabi'. The cartoon character of a below 10-year boy first appeared in the Weekly Bichitra in 1978 during Ziaur Rahman's rule and soon became very popular representing the street urchins or dumpsters and speaking wittily about disparity, hypocrisy, loopholes and ruthlessness of the society. Sheikh Hasina took the name of the character as a representative of all the street children, of them she once personally came across were Mannan and others. However, she expresses strong reservation over the way the word 'Tokai' is used to refer to the street children-"A journalist once threw a question at me – why do we see street children often at political rallies?

By the word children, he meant the little boys and girls who have been given the sad appellation of street urchins. ...I tried to give him the answer I thought would do. But all said and done, the question has remained embedded in me. It has come back over and over again. And I have asked myself why they are called 'Tokai'. That is the way we have used the term, and it has always been a demeaning way. Their birth, way of living, their future, all of these have given a tug at the heart in me. From where have these children come? And why do they make do with life on the streets?" [8]

Throughout her book, Sheikh Hasina shows how government failures have deprived not only the Tokai but millions of other men and women across the country of their basic human rights. It was amazing that she so persuasively outlined the most important solutions, such as abolishing poverty, providing free education and meals for students in schools, and empowering women. These issues were put on the priority agenda of her government, which made phenomenal progress in eradicating poverty, reaching out to school children with free books and meals, empowering women and thus reducing the numbers of street children.

This very first work serves as an indicator of the passion, creativity, values, and vision that characterise her entire literary journey as well resonates with her political aspirations for Bangladesh and its people. While she examines historical, social, and cultural factors combined with politics and government to understand the root causes of helpless children sleeping on the streets and living on trash bins, she also realises that those are the causes of the vast majority of citizens being denied basic rights and living in indignity.

She has written books on a variety of topics, focusing mainly on the rights of people to freedom, democracy, national development, security, and social welfare. As a writer, memoire has always been her favourite topic from the beginning. Her works can generally be divided into three broad categories.

One of the major themes of her work is freedom. Several of her books demonstrate her struggle to free democracy from military or quasi-military rulers and to ensure the sustainable development of the country. These include: Ora Tokai Keno (Why are they street children), Bangladeshe Soiratantrer Jonmo (Bangladesh: The Roots of Autocracy), Samoriktantra Bonam Gonatantra (Martial Law versus Democracy), Biponno Gonatantra Lanchito Manobota (Democracy in Distress Demeaned Humanity), Sohena Manobotar Obomanona (Insufferable is the defilement of humanity) and Living in Tears.

In many of her books she has expressed a philosophy on how to ensure the right to democracy, secularism, and peace for the people of Bangladesh, which is similar to the core elements of her political ideology. Among the books are: Daridro Durikorone Kichu Chinta-Bhabna (Some Thoughts About Poverty Eradication), People and Democracy, Brihat Janagosthir Jonne Unnayan (Development for the Masses) and Democracy Poverty Elimination & Peace.

As an author, she strives to accomplish something greater than just writing a story or presenting her point of views. It is also a hallmark of her writings to reflect a deeper and more meaningful perspective on life. Sada Kalo (Black and White), Sobuj Math Periya (Beyond the Green Field), Sheikh Mujib Amar Pita (My Father Sheikh Mujib) and Amader Choto Russel Sona (Our Beloved Little Russell) are some of the works that lead us to that direction.

CHAPTER THREE

In her writings she conveys a philosophy on how to guarantee development, democracy, secular values and peace.

THE EARLY 1980s was a pivotal period for her as she steered her party and guided the people of Bangladesh toward restoring and establishing democracy, which had been absent since 1975. This movement led to clashes with the authorities. She was detained many times and survived several attempts on her life. However, in the 1986 parliamentary elections, her party secured the second-highest number of seats in the national parliament. It was widely believed that Sheikh

Hasina's Awami League would form the government with a comfortable victory if the election had been free and fair.

The election was highly controversial and was labelled by international observers as "a tragedy for democracy". After the elections, Sheikh Hasina was elected the leader of the oppositions and led the movements that ended martial law in Bangladesh. It was during this period when she focused her political campaign on several key issues, including end of military rule, restoration of democracy and elimination of poverty, which is also evident in the writings from this time. She denounces martial law as unconstitutional, which was incorporated into Bangladesh's constitution to legitimise the governments that were formed by military and quasi-military rulers after 1975: "Martial law is nothing more than a law that is imposed through constitutional violations.

Unfortunately, the unconstitutional act of capturing state power is incorporated into the constitution in a bid to legitimise it. And this is what General Zia and General Ershad had done to manipulate the country's political system…..In the Zia-Ershad story, their operating styles were similar. Observing the roots and functioning of the political parties they formed during certain stages of their dictatorships brings home this fact." [9]

In 1990, she led the historic mass movement that culminated in the fall of the Ershad regime. Together with millions of others, Sheikh Hasina celebrated the fall of the autocratic regime as a historical landmark and the start of a new chapter in the nation's history: "The handover of power after toppling an unconstitutional government through a democratic movement was a unique event. The power that had been seized by force of arms, coup d'etats, and other unconstitutional means was finally giving way to the democratic process of statecraft. It was one of the most intrepid instances of struggle in the history of the Bengali nation." [10]

When the pro-democracy movement drove the military regime from power in December 1990, Sheikh Hasina again became the leader of the opposition parties in the national parliament. Her political mission during this period was notable for two most important reasons. As the leader of the oppositions in parliament, she steered an all-out movement towards changing the presidential system of government into a parliamentary one. Outside parliament, she led a mass movement against the BNP's election fraud that resulted in dissolving Khaleda Zia's government. Similarly, she in her writings advocates that the government must be formed solely by the people's mandate, which had been absent in Bangladesh after Bangabandhu's assassination: "Any changes to government must come from the people's mandate, otherwise no one will care about the welfare of the masses or their effective development.... Following the farcical election (15 February 1996), Khaleda's government was forced to resign after a month and a half on 30 March. Since then, no vote-rigging has occurred, and the situation has greatly improved. In order to keep improving, more people need to be informed and aware of their rights." [11]

Her writings promote establishing a global culture of democracy that ensures not only the rule of law but also accountability and transparency within governments. "It is my strong belief that governments across the globe must forcefully implement democracy and justice. Besides, I hope that the governing system will be accountable and transparent." [12]

For her, Bengali nationalism is very important, and she has courageously defended her heritage and culture in the face of incidents that undermine Bengali culture. An example can be found in one of her books where she describes an international event held in Dhaka in 2003 when the BNP-Jamaat alliance government brought the entire nation to disgrace. "The Conference of the Commonwealth Parliamentary Association was inaugurated in Dhaka on 7 October 2003. Conventionally, the inaugural ceremony should begin with the national anthem of the host country. An announcement over the microphone was made. The guests stood up to show respect. ....There was no beginning of our national anthem, only the last line was played— Ami Noyon Jole Bhashi (My eyes are filled with tears). The Khaleda-Nizami government left the nation's eyes filled with tears. What audacity! Dishonour to the national anthem! Guests at the session kept standing but the national anthem was not played. They put the country in a very embarrassing, demeaning and shameful position." [13]

In her early years, Sheikh Hasina observed her father's fight against the same humiliation the Pakistani ruler brought upon the Bengali nation as well as its divide-and-rule policy that benefitted select groups, depriving the masses. She witnessed again how the post-75 quasi-military regimes sought to restore Bangladesh to its pre-independence days. Throughout her writings, she has charted and documented the crisis and the challenges facing the people of Bangladesh, as well as demonstrated her commitment to ensuring the people enjoy a sustained democracy and development. She became more concerned about the country's deteriorating political, social, and economic situations as she travelled across Bangladesh for party meetings and rallies. "My heart and soul take in the realities of life in this land — all the accumulated sadness — as I travel from hamlet to village, from town to city, all across Bangladesh." [14]

Throughout her political career, Sheikh Hasina has been devoted to the welfare of rural people. Her writings follow a similar approach. Having come from a rural background herself, she is familiar with rural life, the life of the majority of the people in Bangladesh; and is aware that the rural people feed the nation by growing grains and vegetables, raising poultry and farming fish. Yet these people have been struggling for generations to escape the traps of poverty and hunger, not to mention the lavish lifestyle they see from a distance in big cities and towns where wealth accumulation shows extreme disparities between urban and rural developments. She saw how the military rulers of post-75 did little for the rural people but initiated some ridiculous and ineffectual initiatives like digging canals; and took poster-perfect photoshoots for propaganda to stay in power.

Also, a self-styled Palli Bandhu (Friend of Rural Bengal) lived in a fortified palatial house in the cantonment, full of comfort, luxury, and enjoyment, while millions of people across the country suffered from his misrule. "As I travelled around different places on foot, by boats and by car, my consolation was helping people at the end and witnessing their struggle closely. I was deeply touched by the pictures, even though they were not spectacular or eye-catching. It was only heart-breaking. I wonder when the day will come for the people of this country to finally end their poverty, agony, famines, and unbearable hardship." [15]

Having personally dealt with ordinary people's hardships, she expresses grave concern in both her politics and writings about how government misrule has left thousands of citizens in utter poverty on the streets of cities and towns far away from their villages. "On my way home from work, I came across some families who had taken refuge on the pavement adjacent to Khamarbari. There were women with their babies as well as young and old men. This scene left me stunned and hurt. It is inappropriate to call them human beings. Instead, they should be called living skeletons. I asked my driver to slow down. As all of them gathered around my car, it had already come to a halt. My purse always contains some cash, so that if someone extends a hand for assistance, they do not go empty-handed. As my conscience always drives me to think in such a manner, I also feel a strong sense of guilt. Both I and they were born on this planet. Even so, there is a vast gap between those of us with cars and these hapless multitudes living in limitless poverty and deprivation on the streets." [16]

There is no wonder that Bangladesh has become a global model for poverty alleviation, female empowerment, combating terrorism, building climate resilience, and digitisation under her leadership. In her writings, she links these issues to the nation's development and progress. Following in Bangabandhu's footsteps who introduced micro-credit to poor, Sheikh Hasina launched her poverty eradication programme which eventually led to a significant drop in poverty rates: "My government introduced micro-credit programs along with skill development training by several ministries. These programs meet the specific needs of particular groups such as the young people, poor women without assets and land, women who sell labour on road construction, and so on. ..There is no unique proven way to one size fits for all type micro-credit and poverty alleviation programs." [17]

Among her other convictions, she has written extensively about the regimes exploiting people's emotions, including using religion to consolidate power and undermining minority faith groups, which she contends is against the core values of Islam. Sheikh Hasina profoundly noted that Bangladesh got independence through a nine-month war fought by its people, irrespective of their religious beliefs. After 1975, constitutional secularism was dropped, which she criticised for disregarding the spirit of the 1971 War of Independence. "The Muslims, Hindus, Christians, and Buddhists fought shoulder-to-shoulder during our great War of Liberation to bring us independence. For their sacrifice to never be undermined, the Constitution included secularism as a pillar. Secularism aims to eradicate bigotry from society so people can live together peacefully. However, secularism was later removed from the Constitution without explanation."[18]

In her works, Sheikh Hasina demonstrates her commitment to fight against fundamentalism, militancy, and terrorism. At the same time, her religious belief remains very clear. There are many articles in her books that express this perspective where she clarifies that her life is guided by the Holy Quran and that true Islam never condones terrorism or repression. "…being a Muslim, I must abide by the dictates of the Holy Book. Islam is a religion of peace and humanity. The true believers of Islam do not and cannot support the repression of human beings, or terrorism and terrorist activities." [19]

Bringing the killers of 15 August 1975 to justice was the most challenging task Sheikh Hasina's government had undertaken when it took office in 1996. For Sheikh Hasina, as she explains, the August 15 assassination was far more than a personal tragedy- it had deep historical roots. Her account on this is a brilliant example of high-quality literature and accurate interpretation of historical backgrounds. She writes: "Once again, that 15 August 1975 witnessed the betrayal of the hopes and aspirations of the people of this soil. Recall 1757, on the field of Plassey where that other grand betrayal enslaved the Bengali people for two centuries, when Bengal's last independent Nawab, Sirajuddowla, was treacherously let down by his commander-in-chief. Here in newly independent, war-torn Bangladesh, Khondokar Mostaque's lust for power to become the president of this country, led him to murder Bangabandhu with the collusion and collaboration of his trusted boys Col Rashid, Col Faruq, Major Dalim, Huda, Shahriar, Mohiuddin, Khairuzzaman, Mohsin and others. And just as on that field of Plassey two hundred years ago, the soldiers of Sirajuddowla refused to defend him at the behest of that other traitor Mir Jafar, who had lusted for power, to replace Sirajuddowla. Among those who had betrayed Bangabandhu were some of his most trusted people, some who had been moulded by his own hands and had reached the heights of power due to the reflected glory of Bangabandhu.

Strangely, history is full of repetition. However, we never learn from history. So, for instance, Mir Jafar could not withstand the bitter fruit of the treachery he committed (he was Nawab for just three months), our Mostaque was president of Bangladesh for not even three months! Traitors are not trusted wholly, even by their evil masters. Such is history!... Through the assassinations of August 1975, a government elected by the people was put to flight, and in its place was initiated the first of many attempts to govern the country on the strength of illegitimacy." [20]

A promise Sheikh Hasina made to herself on her return from exile was that she would bring to justice those who killed her father, mother, brothers, and many others. Consequently, the 15 August killers were sentenced to death during her first term, and the final verdict was delivered in November 2009, less than a year after she came to power for the second time. For this, her tribute is monumental to all the people of Bangladesh who inspired and provided her with the strength necessary to accomplish this hard task, including freedom fighters, writers, academics, journalists, cultural activists, and social workers. In one of her books, Sheikh Hasina explained how the words of eminent writer Shaheed Janoni (Mother of Martyr) Begum Jahanara Imam provided her with inspiration during a difficult time: "Begum Jahanara Imam is no longer alive. She left us on 26 June (1994). She led our spirits to greater awareness.

With her magical inspirational personality, she reinforced our inner courage, which was crucial for our country and nation. ..As I read her book Ekattorer Dingulee (The days of 1971), all the descriptions came alive for me. During that time, I and my family, including my mother, sister Rehana, and brothers Jamal and Russell, were being held captive by Pakistani soldiers inside a house in Dhaka. We saw and experienced the torture of the invading forces on people. The captivity was like death cell until we heard the sounds of our freedom fighters at actions. The sound of bombings and gunfires was our lifeblood during that time. The freedom fighters have carried out several operations on that road.

During their operations, the extent of torture on us would increase. Our lights were turned off in the evening. Foods could not be bought or cooked. When we sat down for dinner, Pakistani forces brandishing weapons through the windows ordered us- Stop eating and turn off the lights. You don't need to have any more food." [21]

The execution of the 15 August killers marked the accomplishment of her commitment and the defeat of the conspirators who had delayed it since 1975: "Many governments were toppled through such recourse, but never were the killers tried in law courts, whereas in Bangladesh the normal laws have tried the killers, and they have been sentenced to death. These condemned ones also have their foreign sanctuary. The head of one such state wrote me a letter with a request to pardon the killers. He even referred to particular verses from the holy Quran which exhorts pardon. In my reply, quoting from the same holy book (Al Quran), I had mentioned the responsibilities of children towards their parents, and what should be their attitude toward the killers of their fathers and what guidelines the holy book had for this and to follow the imperatives of those uidelines." [22]

Consequently, she not only brought the August killers to justice but also established an International Crimes Tribunal (ICT) to prosecute those who committed crimes against humanity during the liberation war. Several verdicts have been given and executed by the tribunal, following its investigation and prosecution of suspected war criminals. Some quarters attempted to undermine the prosecution by propagating the false claim that Bangabandhu had declared general clemency to collaborators of the Pakistani forces. Sheikh Hasina drew a strong conclusion against this: "Based on a triparty agreement, the Awami League announced a general amnesty to free some 400,000 Bengalis from Pakistan's prisons. Their family members and relatives gathered in the streets with tearful eyes to appeal to Bangabandhu to free and take back their fathers, brothers, and husbands from Pakistan's jails. Against this backdrop, Bangabandhu granted clemency, and subsequently, the captive Bengalis including (former military chief) General Nuruddin, (former BDR chief) General Latif, General Mahmudul Hasan, General Salam and many others were able to return home….. Additionally, people who were part of various groups collaborating with Pakistani forces, but discreetly provided shelter to freedom fighters to carry out guerrilla attacks during the liberation war, were also granted clemency. Those who committed war crimes like genocide, lootings, rape of women, and setting fire to peoples' houses were not granted amnesty in general." [23]

Along with this kind of propaganda, she fought against anti-liberation forces' bid to destroy the history, heritage, and traditions of the Bengali nation.

Since the nationality of the people of Bangladesh was changed to 'Bangladeshi' from 'Bengali', her writings serve as a forceful reminder that the people of Bangladesh fought for independence as Bengalis rather than as Bangladeshis. Sheikh Hasina insists that the word Bangladeshi means 'Made in Bangladesh' or 'Produce from Bangladesh' but is not a definition of nationality. To address another argument, which claims that Bengali speakers of all nationalities are Bengalis, she asserts: "In our neighbouring country India, there is a substantial Bengali speaking population who identifies themselves as Indian. The Americans are not English, even though they speak English. English is spoken in many other countries, including Australia and Canada, where people don't claim to be English." [24]

The first time Sheikh Hasina became prime minister was on June 23, 1996, after her party Bangladesh Awami League won the general elections held on June 12, 1996. From 1996 to 2001, she led the country to great socioeconomic successes and achieved a great deal in many areas. Among them are diplomatic triumphs in solving long-standing bilateral issues with India, including the 30-year Ganges Water Sharing Treaty. She also established peace in the Chittagong Hill tracts and pursued the trials of Bangabandhu's killers. The peace process that ended a three-decade insurgency in the country's southeast hill districts is an example of her most challenging work in terms of establishing peace.: "Khagachari Stadium witnessed a historic event on February 10 (1997). On that day, the stadium as well as the entire hill district were adorned with a festive look in celebration of the surrender of weapons by the Shantibahini (insurgents). The peace process drew enormous attention not only in Bangladesh but from around the world as well.

On this occasion, diplomats, development agency representatives, political leaders, intellectuals, poets, writers, journalists, artists and cultural activists were present. A huge crowd gathered there as well. Many were sceptical about the surrender of arms by the insurgents. ….. Jana Samghati Samiti chief Jyotirindra Narayan Larma alias Santu Larma, however, handed me weapons on behalf of the Shantibahini. I greeted him with fresh white roses, then released white pigeons to symbolize lasting peace." [25]

At the same time, there was significant development of the infrastructure with grand projects, such as the construction of the Bangabandhu Bridge. Her other initiatives included helping distressed, landless, and deprived people, introducing beneficial programmes for farmers, and social safety nets for the poorest in society. She introduced allowances for disadvantaged women, widows, the disabled, and freedom fighters as well as the Ashrayan (Shelter) programme for the homeless.

Taking action based on self-recommendations is an example of being honest.

As for the conspiracy to obliterate the actual history and spirit of the 1971 War of Independence, Sheikh Hasina's greatest concern has always been the security of the country. The extent to which she has thought about this important issue may be seen in her writings about how Bangabandhu had established and started the modernisation of the Bangladesh Army after independence, as well as how he envisioned a disciplined security force for the country. She asserts Bangabandhu wanted the army to be the friend of the people, not a counterforce like those of the military under West Pakistan's dominance before Independence.

After 1975, however, the cult of power-mongering army officers established anti-liberation tyrannies, which shattered his vision. Sheikh Hasina also disputed propaganda about Bangabandhu's attitude towards the army during that period, citing references to his efforts to reorganise and modernise Bangladesh Army as a strong security force and the front-line workers in rebuilding the war-torn country: "Bangabandhu had prepared his plan for rebuilding and developing the Bangladesh armed forces in just three and a half years when the newly independent country was experiencing various challenges. During this period, economic restructuring and rehabilitation were the most urgent calls. Despite the challenges, Bangabandhu pursued initiatives and activities for ensuring the welfare and progress of the armed forces." [26]

Under the BNP-Jamaat rule, Sheikh Hasina witnessed with despair how the armed forces were manipulated by power-grabbing parties, which were supposed to be the people's friends. When it comes to protecting their position in power, they even put the army in a very controversial position: "At a time when the overall law and order situation was so critical, the government of the BNP-Jamaat Alliance summoned in the military at night throughout the country on October 16, 2002. It was the first time that a government responsible to parliament invited the military to assist the civil government... The Alliance Government sparked a confrontation between the military and the people. They have destroyed the relationship of trust, confidence, and hope that the military had with the civilians. In the course of Operation Clean Heart, news of one death after another poured in. It was then stated on behalf of the Government that nobody died of torture; the people died of heart failure." [27]

Sheikh Hasina won the 2008 election again with a landslide victory when the people of Bangladesh mandated her to free the nation from oppression, tortures, hunger, and endless conspiracy to undermine the values and spirit of the 1971 War of Independence. Since then, she has led the country to reduce poverty, empower women, strengthen climate resilience, boost international trade, create large-scale labour market opportunities through digitisation, and raise Bangladesh from the Least Developed Countries (LDCs) category to lower middle income status. Providing shelter to over a million displaced Myanmar citizens, the Rohingyas, she shows her courage and commitment to humanity that is passionately expressed in her writings.

CHAPTER FOUR

It is also a hallmark of her writings to reflect a deeper and more meaningful perspective on life.

IN HER WRITINGS, she does not just express political views, but a greater and deeper understanding of life. There are many moving accounts of her own personal story. She candidly reflects on her rural and urban upbringing in her writings. In the way she recalls an experience from her childhood, we see how the personality and determination ingrained in her since childhood. 'My father had a female cousin barely four years older than me.

That aunt used to take all the little ones of our home to school. We were to cross a small canal over a bamboo bridge. On the first day, I was terrified to cross that bridge. My aunt held my hand and gave me the courage to cross the bridge as I trembled in fear. From then on, I was never afraid to cross the bridge. In fact, I used to be the first one to cross it." [28]

A reflection on her first day of college illustrates a similar urban example. Sheikh Hasina expected a day of joy and excitement and was pleased to be studying with her new friends. However, an upsetting experience occurred which was etched on her mind. On the day, she was wearing a white shalwar and a printed kameez in a light paste shade; one of her favourite colours. While she and other newcomers entered the college, some senior students poured coloured water on them in ragging. Her new dress turned red and her spectacles were soaked. She has written down what happened next: "There was a classmate next to me. I dropped all my books into her hands as I glanced ahead at the buckets full of coloured water. The seniors were taking water out of those buckets to pour on others. Taking my time, I walked towards the buckets when I was drenched by water being thrown on me. Yet, I didn't stop them nor protest. However, it was the first blow that took me a few moments to recover from. Despite my discomfort, I walked towards them, smiling like I was having fun, too. In time, I reached a bucket and raised it to throw water on them. My counterattack came as a complete surprise to them." [29]

It was a revealing response from the future leader of Bangladesh. While in intermediate college, she had initially entered the field of politics and won an election to become vice president of the college students' union (the principal was the de facto president). She also served as the secretary and subsequently the president of the college unit of Students' League, the nation's leading student organisation.

During her tenure, she led a movement calling for the construction of a *Shaheed Minar* (Martyr Monument) on campus, which was no easy feat during Pakistan's rule. The college principal turned down the request for the monument but Sheikh Hasina encouraged a group of students to build a makeshift *Shaheed Minar*, using bricks from a construction site. She recalled the memory in her writings: "Since the college was undergoing construction work, we gathered bricks from there, piled one on top of the other and constructed a Shaheed Minar, where we paid tribute to our martyrs by laying flowers. This happened on the 20th of February. The next day was the 21st of February. After college, we gathered together for the *Ekushey* Rally in the evening. As soon as our Principal got to hear about it, she came and dismantled the Shaheed Minar at night. The next day the college remained closed. Even though, we went to the college and paid respect in the empty place." [30]

As the students' movement gained momentum, the principal of the college informed the District Commissioner (DC) of Dhaka about the protest and threatened Sheikh Hasina with arrest and imprisonment. She responded to the threat with courage: "My father was in jail then, and Nazimuddin Road (where the central jail was located) was not far from Bakshi Bazar (where her college was). The Rickshaw fare would be four *annas* (a quarter of a Taka). After every 15 days, I got a chance to meet my father, and I would go there from my college quite often. Therefore, when they threatened that I would be put behind bars, I said that I had no objection." [31]

When the DC visited the college, Sheikh Hasina and her fellow students surrounded him as he stepped out of the principal's room. After a brief discussion, he agreed to their demands and suggested they contact him to discuss the arrangement of building the *Shaheed Minar*. Sheikh Hasina went to the DC's office along with the general secretary of the college students' union and some other students. During discussions, the DC offered Sheikh Hasina the opportunity to meet with her father, who was in jail. It was an attempt to divert attention from the main issue of discussion. Sheikh Hasina realised the DC wanted to stop them from building the monument, but she continued to fight for it. Later, she declined to sign the college budget because it did not include funding for the martyrs' monument. The principal detained her for around five hours as a punishment. The college authorities eventually gave in and built the monument, marking one of Sheikh Hasina's first successful campaigns. In some ways, it heralded the beginning of her career as a political activist. "In this college, I was elected to the post of Vice President (of the students' union) with a landslide. My political career started from this college and is continuing," she later wrote. (32)

Not only was this the beginning of her political career, it was also the beginning of a lifetime journey in which her experiences made an indelible mark on her writings, providing a deeper level of understanding than any belief or ideology. The enduring memory she describes in her books illustrates this essence of life. "Tungipara village in Gopalganj district used to be on the bank of the Madhumati River but now it is far (because the river is narrowing due to low water flows). Nowadays, Baiger, a branch of Madhumati, serenely flows alongside the village. Its waters glitter like silver on a sunny day as well as a moonlit night. On both sides of the Baiger were *Kashbans* (a native grass that blooms in a snow-white flowers during autumn), fields of paddy, jute, and sugarcane, date, palm, coconut and *amloki* (amla) trees, as well as bamboo and banana bushes and numerous wild shrubs and a blanket of green grass. It was a picturesque landscape in which endless chirping of sparrows, *shaliks*, and the sound of doves on a lazy afternoon made one fall in love with it. When I was born in my village Tungipara, it was a sun kissed Ashwin (autumn) afternoon. My childhood was spent in this village blessed with the beauty and tranquillity of nature and the simplicity of rural life." (33)

This was written in 1986, shortly before her 40th birthday. Bangladesh was ruled by the dictatorial Ershad government at the time, and the political and social climate in the country was oppressive. However, it took a long time before people realised that only a mass movement could restore democracy and save them from oppression akin to Pakistan. As Sheikh Hasina endured the crisis, sweet memories comforted and rejuvenated her. She evokes a vivid scene of lush green fields, a moonlit night, twinkling stars above, birds chirping at sunrise over paddy fields, and the peace of nature. Growing up in rural Bengal, she enjoyed muddy water during the monsoon, sweet sun of wintertime, scent of grass, dewdrops, and fireflies glowing in the dark. She liked to drench herself in rain, play on dusty village roads, pick fruits, pluck flowers, and create garlands from flowers found in the jungles and bushes. – "Early in the morning, a group of us little ones walked along the riverbank, and on a winter day, I was thrilled to dip my feet in the warm waters of the river. I would float two coconuts in the river or swim holding onto a banana trunk. The joy of catching small fishes, such as *Tangra* and *punti*, was great. We would dig out *koi* and *byne* fishes from the roots of water hyacinth during monsoon. I was once frightened when I saw a snake up close….

During the hot summer month of *Boishakh*, I would pick a green mango, slice it up into tiny pieces, then combine it with mustard and green chilli. The next step was to wrap it in a banana leaf cone and then suck the juice out of the narrow end. What a delight! Though so many years have passed, I still remember that thrill. If you have never eaten spiced green mango in a banana leaf cone, you won't understand its delight. When wrapped in a banana leaf, mango's aroma was utterly different. What a fight we would have over green mangoes! It would be a scramble to catch the fruits after we shake the branches of the *boroi* tree. In the centre of the village, there was a large *boroi* tree next to the big pond. Often, when we shook it, the reddest looking fruit would land on the water of the pond and nobody could grab it! For not getting the fruit, I would still long for it." (34)

While in reality, she was trying to change the traditional lifestyle and ambience of rural Bangladesh: "I would like to see the village the way it used to be when I was a child. However, that is just a dream because the villages are changing today. Rural life has been changed by machines; everywhere there is the obvious impact of consumerism. Things are now moving at a faster pace than before and even the ordinary village is habituated to the pace of life. Advanced technology is for lightening labour and developing village life is a reality in affluent nations; we must advance too." (35)

It is now easy to reach most of the villages including Tungipara by car and bus from Dhaka. She, however, still finds the village intriguing. There is a particularly moving passage as Sheikh Hasina reminds us of her father's dream of spending his last days with her in their Tungipara village, surrounded by natural beauty. Bangabandhu, the greatest Bengali of all time, who cared deeply about the welfare of the country's people, wished to be among common people in his old age. Sheikh Hasina explained that she could not forget this dream of her father and said the Tungipara village always beacons her: "The pullback of my father's shrine in rural tranquillity draws me there over and over again wherever I am in the world." (36)

The natural beauty and the rich culture of Bangladesh are prominent themes in her works: "The hectic world of public life keeps me very busy, but I still manage to go to Tungipara from time to time. My secret longing is to return to the village of my childhood. My heart yearns to join the poet and sing, even though I can no longer see the dirt road in the distance: *Gram chara oi ranga matir path/ Amaar mon bhulay re* (My king's road that lies still before my house makes my heart wistful- a translation by Rabindranath Tagore)". (37)

She clearly has a deep affection for rural life as she wishes to spend her last days in her village home, leaving behind the conveniences of urban life: "I hope to spend my last days in Tungipara, building a house along the river there is my dream. I would also like to write a memoir about my parents". (38)
Her desire is a remnant of her father's affection: "One of his (Bangabandhu) words keeps coming back to me these days. Often, he told me: 'I will spend my last days in the village (Tungipara) and you will take care of me." (39)

As she reflects on the day Bangabandhu returned from Pakistan, we are reminded of how deeply she missed her father: "The 8th of January (1972) was the most awaited day (for us). In all corners of the globe, news broke that Sheikh Mujib had been released from Pakistani custody and had arrived in London. At night, he called, but we were unable to talk much. I managed to say 'Abba' only once while holding back tears. My mother told my father to return home right away. Finally, the most long-awaited day arrived. On 10 January 1972, our beloved father returned home to his much-loved motherland. Before meeting his family, the people's leader rushed to his people in the Suhrawardi Udyan. He then came home and went immediately to his parents and said salaam to them. Afterward, he met my mother, and within seconds, he embraced her. This was a moment I'll never forget. The hug seemed to last forever. What a great reunion after so much sacrifice and time! As a matter of fact, they were together even on the day they were brutally assassinated on 15 August 1975." [40]

Bangabandhu has been the most important person in Sheikh Hasina's life since her childhood. When she was a young rural girl, she did not want her father to leave the house. So, Bangabandhu tried to sneak out at night only after Sheikh Hasina had gone to bed, to avoid her tears: "I would leave home at night since Hasina would not stop crying if she saw me going away." [41]

Through her works, Sheikh Hasina often reflected on this intense father-daughter relationship. "My father was detained immediately after Ayub Khan declared martial law in 1958. After nearly one and a half years in prison, he was released, but politics was still prohibited. Therefore, he began working for an insurance company when my mother built a two-bedroom house for us in Dhanmondi. We moved to this house (from Segun Bagicha) on October 1, 1961. The first time we had all been able to see him at home for a long time. He would drop me off at school every day before driving to work on (today's) Bangabandhu Avenue. Having my father drive me to school felt like a dream." [42]

However, as Bangabandhu became more involved in politics, he found himself with less time to spend with his family. It became common for him to leave his family for many days. This is how he explained the situation: "I came to Gopalganj this time during a hearing. As usual, when I was there, I would have food sent from our home. I had told my folks to have some eggs sent for me since lack of good food had weakened me considerably. In a month, I had lost a lot of weight. Ranu warned me not to forget that I had once suffered from a heart problem. I tried to tell her I would be fine. What else could I do? Hasina just wouldn't let go of me this time, too. Nowadays, whenever it was time for her to leave, she would burst into tears." [43]

In the same way, Bangabandhu was a broken man when his two daughters left for Germany in 1975. It was a hot and humid day on Wednesday, 30 July 1975. Sheikh Hasina, her sister Sheikh Rehana, and their two children, Saima Wazed Hossain Putul and Sajeeb Wazed Joy, left the country for Germany, just 15 days before the August carnage. A convocation was scheduled for the University of Dhaka on August 15, 1975. The entire university wore a festive look and became ecstatic over the issue. Sheikh Hasina met with DU Vice-Chancellor Dr Abdul Matin Chowdhury before leaving the country. Dr Matin asked her to stay in Dhaka until 15 August to attend the historic convocation. Likewise, Sheikh

Hasina desired that, but she travelled to Germany after her husband who was working there called her. During the departure of his two daughters, Bangabandhu wept like a child. (44)

Her eyes always well up with tears as she remembers the most tragic event in her life: "It would have been better for me if I had stayed in Dhaka and obeyed Sir's (Matin) request... I, too, would have gone with my father, mother, and brothers. I would have been free of my unbearable everyday pain." (45)

Also, Sheikh Hasina has written a touching tribute to her mother on her 91st birthday, which is a classic example of the simple yet poignant style she uses in her writings. Rabindranath Tagore said once, "It is not easy to convey simple ideas in simple words." But Sheikh Hasina seems to have the gift of conveying complex ideas in simple words as she expresses memories that haunt her deeply: "My mother was born in August, as was my brother who was two years younger than me. Her birthday is on the 8th of August (1930); and what a tragedy it was that she was brutally murdered on 15 August (1975). She was married to my father at a very early age and grew up with her many in-laws. I learned a lot about her childhood from my grandpa, grandma, and aunts. As I look back, I recall that my father never stayed home for two years at a time. My mother was surely deprived of a conjugal relationship. Despite this, she never complains, rather believing that her husband works for the welfare of the country and its people. My father bought us a refridgerator from America. She sold it, telling us that drinking chilled water can lead to us catching a cold. In fact, she needed money to support the Awami League's ailing leaders. Sometimes, she could not do the groceries but never told us she had no money. Instead, she cooked *Khicury* (a rice and lentil dish) and served it along with only *Chatni* (a spicy condiment) telling us that taking regular rice dishes every day seemed tasteless. She never shows frustration over a lack of money. I'm her eldest daughter. There wasn't a huge age difference between us. The parents of my mother passed away many years ago. As her eldest daughter, I was like her mother, father, and friend all at the same time. [46]

In the simplicity and clarity of her writing style, she captures the essence of her very personal memory. In this way, her works become universal and timeless. One of the examples of her adept writing style comes from the story of her youngest brother Sheikh Russell: "My father was a huge fan of Bertrand Russell. He would read out Russell's books and explain them to my mother in Bengali, who had become so fascinated with this British philosopher and writer that she named her youngest son after him. ..."He (Russell) was cautious in his movements but brave and barely afraid of anything. He loved playing with big black ants. Once he caught one of those and immediately got a bleeding little finger from its bite. The finger was treated, but it swelled.

Afterwards, he wouldn't catch any ants but gave all of them a common name. When those came into his sight, he would call them Bhutto…..Russell was silenced by the killers' bullets on 15 August 1975. Before being brutally shot, he was forced to wade through the blooded dead bodies of his father, mother, brothers and their wives and uncle. At that moment, watching his beloved ones lying on the floor lifeless, his heart might have pounded to its breaking point in excruciating pain. Why did the killers inflict such pain on Russell and kill him? I wonder if I will ever get an answer to this question." [47]

Her works are characterised by such powerful descriptions that attract readers across the board. One example is when she recounts an incident which happened during a global leaders' conference. "I was clearing my desk (at the G8 Outreach Conference in Italy in 2001) when someone called my name from behind. Turning towards him, I saw he was none other than US President George Bush. I stood up quickly (to greet him) while a front chair fell onto the floor from my sudden motion. Apologising for the incident, I attempted to lift the chair and Mr Bush did the same, but his glasses fell onto the floor. I was holding the chair's legs and Mr Bush was holding its other side. A gentleman offered us assistance but Mr Bush repositioned the chair. He also repeatedly told me, "It's okay, it's okay," when I was so embarrassed for what had happened." [48]

Taking the readers through another poignant passage in which she illustrates the agony of being imprisoned for nearly a year in solitary confinement in 2007 when the army-backed caretaker government was in power: "As I look east from my prison, I can see the parliament. In the north is Ganabhaban. In the mornings and afternoons, I stand at the window to watch people move across the green field. Standing beside the window, I once saw a healthy monkey crossing a green field towards the north. The monkey would come to the northern boundary wall as I hurl food to it two to three times a day. Unusually, it did not stop walking across the field that day. I saw it stopped briefly and glanced around for a moment before continuing, then disappeared into the woods near the lake. Unlike me confined inside a prison, the monkey is free to roam across the field. In a small room on the second floor (of the parliament building), I am in solitary confinement. I couldn't cross the green field at my whim. But no one can stop my mind from going beyond the green field." [49]

Through her life experiences, Sheikh Hasina has learned how to overcome obstacles. She has virtually no bounds in both her literary works and her political career since they capture a remarkable life and nearly every aspect of the nation she loves and serves. And her writing conveys a powerful message that she is committed to Bangladesh's development, particularly for the poorest and most marginalised.

CHAPTER FIVE

THE MAJOR WORKS OF SHEIKH HASINA

The Major Works of Sheikh Hasina

Ora Tokai Keno
Why Are They Street Children
1989

Bangladeshe Soiratantrer Jonmo
Bangladesh: The Roots of Autocracy
1993

Samoriktantra Bonam Gonatantra
Martial Law Versus Democracy
1994

Daridro Durikorone Kichu Chinta-Bhabna
Some Thoughts on Poverty Alleviation
1995

People and Democracy
1997

Brihat Janagosthir Jonne Unnayan
Development for the masses
1999

Biponno Gonatantra Lanchito Manobota
Democracy in Distress Demeaned Humanity
2002

Sohena Manobotar Obomanona
Insufferable is the defilement of humanity
2003

Living in Tears
2004

Democracy Poverty Elimination & Peace
2005

Sada Kalo
Black and White
2007

Sabuj Math Periya
Beyond the green field
2011

Sheikh Mujib Amaar Pita
My Father Sheikh Mujib
2015

Amader Chotto Russell Sona
Our beloved little Russell
2018

My Father My Bangladesh
2021

Ora Tokai Keno
Why Are They Street Children
February 1989

> "The Irony of the situation is that wherever anyone involved in the working of the state— be it a bureaucrat, businessman, teacher, doctor, politician, social worker, intellectual –has spoken at gatherings, the refrain has always been that children are the future of the country. But these children, those I am speaking of, whose birth, life, the struggle for survival all begin and end on the street— what future do they look forward to?"

Bangladeshe Soiratantrer Jonmo
Bangladesh: The Roots of Autocracy
February 1993

"The history of democracy in this part of the world has not been a happy one. Indeed, it was from the beginning of the Pakistani state that democracy has systematically come under the onslaught, repeatedly, to the point where it became well-nigh difficult for the pluralistic process to establish and then consolidate itself."

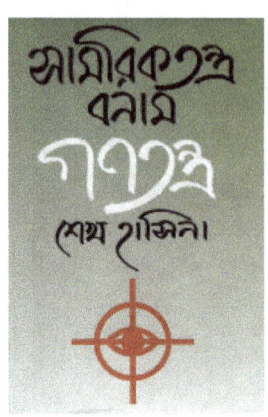

Shamoriktantra Bonam Ganatantra
Martial Law Versus Democracy
February 1994

"When Bangabandhu remained concerted on nation-building activities immediately after independence, he was assassinated to topple a democratically elected government and martial law was imposed in the country. Grabbing power by scheming and killing has become a rite of passage in this nation since then."

***Daridra Durikorone Kichu Chinta-Bhabna*
Some Thoughts on Poverty Alleviation
February 1995**

"Poverty is a multidimensional problem, which means that to end poverty, we need to address multiple factors, including income, employment, housing, education, health, and disaster preparedness. People should be involved in local government activities for increasing awareness and their ability to organise."

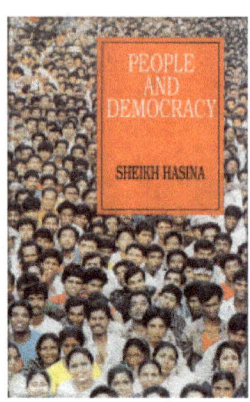

People and Democracy
January 1997

"All human beings are born free and equal in dignity and rights. They are endowed with reason and conscience and should act towards one another in a spirit of brotherhood."

Brihat Janagosthir Jonne Unnayan
Development for the masses
February 1999

"I believe a fundamental change is needed to our politics where competition between parties will be on their plans and programmes for people's welfare. Movements should be for reformation and development not towards the benefit of select groups, but the masses."

***Biponno Gonatantra Lanchita Manobota*
February 2002
Democracy in Distress Demeaned Humanity
English Edition February 2003**

"It is profound sadness which overwhelms my heart when I think about my beloved countrymen. From deep within my soul, I cry out for them. Their sadness, torture, deprivation torment my mind."

Sohena Manobotar Obomanona
**Insufferable is the Defilement of the Humanity
February 2003**

"If any party or group can seize power by the force of muscle, arms or black money, then voters will have no place in such a scheme. It will not take into account the human beings and will turn absolutely autocratic."

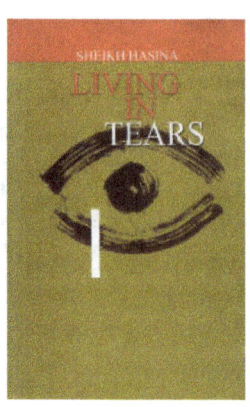

**Living in Tears
January 2004**

"If the amount of money that is spent worldwide for acquiring weapons were spent for children's education and health then it would be possible to restore to every child his rights. If the amount of money that is spent in each war could be used for achieving women's rights and for food and shelter of the world's poor and generating employment then poverty would be banished from the world."

Democracy Poverty Elimination & Peace
February 2005

"While strengthening democracy, I have tried my best to institutionalise it. Unfortunately, democracy got a severe jolt in my own country after national election was announced on October 1, 2001. The non-party caretaker government for which I struggled so hard took a very partisan role and through rigged polls ensured the victory of Bangladesh Nationalist Party and its religious fanatic ally, the Jamat-e-Islami."

Sada Kalo
Black and White
February 2007

"Time and again, the country and its people had suffered to fulfil the desire of many people who wished to be political leaders but lacked the background and knowledge of politics."

Sabuj Math Periya
Beyond the Green Field
February 2011

"My mother loved to read Sufia Kamal's books whenever a new one was published. She told me that my father also enjoyed her writings. It had been my desire to meet Sufia Kamal, and the opportunity finally came. Sufia Kamal's daughter, Lulu, who was my classmate, took me to her home in Tarabag and introduced me to her mother. The first time I saw her seated on the balcony with Kharoms (handmade traditional sandals) on her feet, wearing a sari, preparing fish to be cooked, it was a very special moment. She favoured cooking on her own and my mother as well, especially for my father. Sufia Kamal reminded me of my mother at first glance as both are extremely family-oriented."

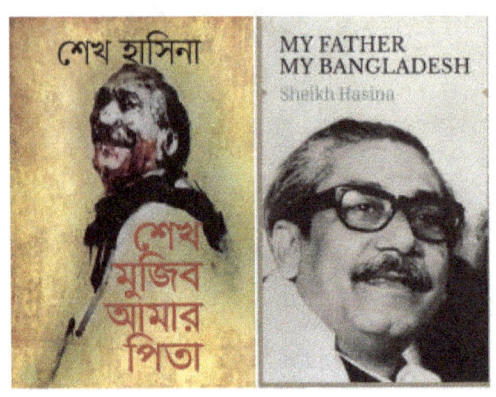

***Sheikh Mujib Amar Pita*
February 2015
My Father, My Bangladesh
English Edition April 2021**

"My days are filled with meetings, lectures, and dealing with hundreds of people. As I go to sleep at night, it's a whole different world. That's my intimate life, the life of nineteen years ago."

Amader Chotto Russell Sona
Our beloved little Russell
March 2018

"Whenever anyone asked him what he wanted to be as an adult, Russell replied, "I would like to be an officer in the army. It was his dream to be in the military. During the War of Independence, he wanted to serve."

REFERENCES

REFERENCES

Chapter One

1. Sheikh Mujib Amar Pita (My Father Sheikh Mujib), pages 58-59
2. Sheikh Mujib Amar Pita (My Father Sheikh Mujib), pages 70-71
3. Sheikh Mujib Amar Pita (My Father Sheikh Mujib), page 57
4. Introductory Remarks, Ora Tokai Keno (Why Are They Street Children)

Chapter Two

5. Brihat Janagosthir Jonne Unnayan (Development for the Masses), page 55
6. The description of the reception and the quotes from Sheikh Hasian's speech have been taken from newspapers reports those appeared on 18 May 1981.
7. Ora Tokai Keno (Why Are They Street Children), pages 55-56
8. Ora Tokai Keno Why Are They Street Children), page 64

Chapter Three

9. Bangladeshe Soiratantrer Jonmo (Bangladesh: The Roots of Autocracy), pages 26-27
10. Bangladeshe Soiratantrer Jonmo (Bangladesh: The Roots of Autocracy), page 11
11. Brihat Janagosthir Jonne Unnayan (Development for the Masses), pages 12-13
12. Democracy, Poverty Elimination and Peace, page 85
13. Living in Tears, pages 44-45
14. Preface by Sheikh Hasina, People and Democracy
15. Bangladeshe Soiratantrer Jonmo (Bangladesh: The Roots of Autocracy), page 37
16. Daridro Durikorone Kichu Chinta-Bhabna (Some Thoughts on Poverty Alleviation) page 11
17. Democracy Poverty Elimination & Peace, page 91
18. Ora Tokai Keno (Why Are They Street Children), page 37
19. Democracy, Poverty Alleviation and Peace, page 68
20. People and Democracy, pages 12 & 27

21. *Daridro Durikorone Kichu Chinta-Bhabna (Some Thoughts on Poverty Alleviation), pages 46-47*
22. *Biponno Gonatantra Lanchito Manobota (Democracy in Distress Demeaned Humanity), page 57*
23. *Shamoriktantra Bonam Ganatantra (Martial Law versus Democracy), pages 89-90*
24. *Ora Tokai Keno (Why are they street children), page 35*
25. *Brihat Janagosthir Jonne Unnayan (Development for the Masses), pages 38 & 40*
26. *Ora Tokai Keno (Why are they street children), page 27*
27. *Sohena Manobotar Obomanona (Insufferable is the defilement of humanity), pages 30, 33 & 34*

Chapter Four

28. *Sheikh Mujib Amar Pita (My Father Sheikh Mujib), page 56*
29. *Biponno Gonatantra Lanchito Manobota (Democracy in Distress Demeaned Humanity) pages 12-13*
30. *Biponno Gonatantra Lanchito Manobota (Democracy in Distress Demeaned Humanity) page 14*
31. *Biponno Gonatantra Lanchito Manobota (Democracy in Distress Demeaned Humanity) pages 14-15*
32. *Biponno Gonatantra Lanchito Manobota (Democracy in Distress Demeaned Humanity) pages 16*
33. *Sheikh Mujib Amar Pita (My Father Sheikh Mujib), page 54*
34. *Sheikh Mujib Amar Pita (My Father Sheikh Mujib), pages 56-57*
35. *Sheikh Mujib Amar Pita (My Father Sheikh Mujib), page 58*
36. *Sheikh Mujib Amar Pita (My Father Sheikh Mujib), page 57*
37. *Sheikh Mujib Amar Pita (My Father Sheikh Mujib), page 58*
38. *Sheikh Mujib Amar Pita (My Father Sheikh Mujib), pages 57-58*
39. *Sheikh Mujib Amar Pita (My Father Sheikh Mujib), page 57*
40. *Sabuj Math Periya (Beyond the Green Field), pages 73, 85*
41. *Oshomapto Attojiboni (The Unfinished Memories) by Sheikh Mujibur Rahman, page 165*
42. *Sada Kalo (Black and White), page 73*
43. *Oshomapto Attojiboni (The Unfinished Memories) by Sheikh Mujibur Rahman, page 185*

44. *The heart-rending departure of Sheikh Hasina and Sheikh Rehana from their father was witnessed by Dr Mohammed Farashuddin in 1975, when he was Bangabandhu's secretary. He recounts the memory in an interview with Bangladesh Sangbad Sangstha (BSS) in 2018.*

45. *Sheikh Mujib Amar Pita (My Father Sheikh Mujib), page 81*

46. *A translation of selected passages from My Mother Sheikh Fazilatun Nesa*

47. *Amader Chotto Russell Sona (Our beloved little Russell), pages 15, 17, 41*

48. *Sada Kalo (Black and White), page 46*

49. *Sabuj Math Periya (Beyond the green field), pages 45-46*

www.ingramcontent.com/pod-product-compliance
Lightning Source LLC
Chambersburg PA
CBHW071538080526
44588CB00011B/1720